LEANNE MORGAN PROSOPOGRAPHY:

What in the World?! Essays and Inspirations

By

Leland Tyler

TABLE OF CONTENTS

INTRODUCTION

The Charm of a Southern Belle

In a world where comedy can often be overwhelming with shock and sarcasm, Leanne Morgan offers a delightful alternative with her humor that exudes Southern charm, genuine authenticity, and a touch of sassy wisdom. Leanne's comedy is a captivating display of storytelling, carefully woven from the rich tapestry of her life as a wife, mother, daughter, and friend. For years, she has been mesmerizing audiences with a diverse array of stories, exploring everything from the peculiarities of dieting trends to the surprising complexities of friendships in middle age. Her stories are brimming with humor and relatability, connecting with the universal experiences that unite us. From the awkwardness of navigating adolescence to the joys and struggles of raising children, from the complexities of aging to the personal struggles of finding one's voice in a bustling society.

Leanne's journey to becoming a beloved comedian is far from the typical tale of overnight fame or chances in a bustling city. Her journey was shaped by her resolute determination, steadfast conviction, and a finely-tuned sense of humor that has guided her through life's unforeseen obstacles. Leanne, a native of rural Tennessee, never expected to find herself pursuing a career in comedy. Contrary to popular belief, she had a humble upbringing as the daughter of a butcher, immersed in the stories of a close-knit community and the practical

6

wisdom that comes from living a simple yet meaningful life. It was in this modest Southern town that she began to see the world through a mixture of amusement and modesty.

Leanne's ascent in the comedy world was anything but expected. Despite the industry's focus on cutting-edge and urban trends, Leanne, a woman in her fifties with a delightful Southern accent and a genuine love for her audience, exceeded all expectations. She achieved success by staying true to herself, rather than seeking attention through controversy or loudness. Her comedy was deeply rooted in the genuine and relatable moments of everyday life, the type of stories that are exchanged during a family gathering with a lighthearted smile and heartfelt laughter.

Her early shows were held in cozy settings, particularly living rooms, where she entertained groups of women who had come together for jewelry parties. Throughout these occasions, she not only recounted her experiences but also offered her handmade jewelry for sale. Unbeknownst to her, these informal gatherings provided the ideal setting for refining her comedic talents and nurturing her distinctive voice. Here, surrounded by women who embodied a range of roles and relationships, Leanne honed her sharp observation skills, empathy, and ability to connect with others. It wasn't solely about bringing joy to others; it was about fostering a deep sense of understanding and connection.

Leanne's comedy is deeply personal, drawing inspiration from her life with Chuck, her husband who has a completely different personality, her journey as a mother to three children, and her evolving role as a modern Southern woman. She fearlessly delves into subjects that are often considered taboo in polite discussions—struggles with body image, the intricacies of marriage, the ups and downs of hormonal fluctuations, and the importance of finding comfort in undergarments. However, what distinguishes her is not just the subjects she covers, but rather the manner in which she presents them. Leanne's personal stories have a remarkable ability to connect with individuals from diverse backgrounds, surpassing age and cultural differences. There's something truly enchanting about her storytelling, with her Southern charm and a twinkle in her eye that brings an extra touch of magic. Her humor is designed to uplift and gently remind us that laughter can be the best remedy for life's most perplexing moments.

Her story also explores finding purpose in the later years of life, a journey that connects with audiences who often feel overlooked or unappreciated by mainstream society. For many years, Leanne struggled to discover her true self beyond her roles as a wife and mother. Comedy became her way of expressing her unique perspective, embracing the vibrant and unpredictable beauty of life. Leanne's charm lies in her genuine nature, as she doesn't pretend to have all the answers. Instead, she invites her audience to discover the humor in the absurdities of life: the futile diets, the unfaithful friends, the exasperating spouses, and the surprising transformations our bodies undergo as we grow older.Leanne Morgan Prosopography: What in the World?! Essays and Inspirations" provides much more than a collection of entertaining stories. Step into Leanne's extraordinary world, where laughter and authentic emotions blend together, inviting you to immerse yourself completely. It's about embracing oneself and the present circumstances, and having the courage to find laughter in the midst of uncertainty. Within these pages, readers will find a rich source of inspiration, comfort, and plenty of laughter, all delivered with Leanne's unique Southern charm that has made her a well-known figure in the comedy world. As we delve into this exploration of her life and thoughts, we are reminded that whenever we come across moments of confusion or bewilderment, there is an opportunity to uncover happiness, connection, and a hint of enchantment amidst the disorder.

CHAPTER 1

Uncovering the Sense of Humor –

The Early Years

Leanne Morgan's comedic journey started in a unique environment, far from the flashy world of comedy clubs or busy city stages. It began in a humble setting - in the heart of rural Tennessee, in a small town where everyone knew each other, and daily life centered around front porch conversations and church events. She came into the world as part of a family that valued hard work, good manners, and a positive outlook on life. Leanne's childhood was shaped by her father's profession as a butcher, which exposed her to a lively community of unique individuals. These individuals were full of vibrant personalities that could instantly light up a room, much like their captivating stories could fill a pot of stew. Here, in this humble corner of America, Leanne discovered her initial audience and began to understand the power of storytelling.

Leanne's father, the local butcher, was a talented multitasker who could effortlessly slice a pork chop while captivating his audience with his stories. From behind the meat counter, he would engage customers with his quick wit and warm personality, turning the mundane chore of grocery shopping into a vibrant social interaction. Leanne carefully observed and acquired knowledge. She observed the way her father's keen intellect and natural charm effortlessly fostered a warm and inviting environment, how his stories could bring laughter and comfort during challenging times. This is where Leanne first experienced the magic of comedy—the ability of a well-timed joke to break the ice, relieve tension, and forge connections. These initial lessons formed the basis for her future career, even if she may not have been aware of it at the time.

Having grown up in this close-knit community, Leanne developed her own unique perspective on life. She found joy in the simple things, finding humor in the everyday moments that often go unnoticed. She closely studied the behavior of people at church socials, the way they whispered gossip at the beauty parlor, and how they joyfully shared their family's achievements as if they were their own. Leanne's developing comedic sensibility drew inspiration from the idiosyncrasies, paradoxes, everyday pleasures, and subtle heartaches of rural communities.

However, it wasn't just the adults who shaped her sense of humor; the children she grew up with also had a major impact. Leanne was a quiet child, often preferring to observe rather than actively engage. She developed a keen eye for detail and a talent for mimicking others. She found herself gravitating towards the more extroverted and charismatic children, quietly observing their actions and later recounting her own interpretations of their experiences. She began to understand that humor could act as a shield against life's challenges, while also helping her forge meaningful connections with others. From an early age, she grasped the deep influence of humor on people's emotions, its power to go beyond the mundane, and its potential to bring people together.

Leanne's intelligence began to flourish during her time in school. Despite not being known as the class clown, she had a talent for delivering witty, hushed comments that always managed to elicit laughter from her friends. She possessed a deep understanding of social dynamics, knowing exactly when to speak up and when to stay quiet. Her sense of humor was more subtle and understated. Instead, it was characterized by cleverness, keen observation, and frequently surprising insights. She didn't need the limelight to leave a lasting impression, a trait that would later influence her performance on stage.

Leanne's storytelling skills blossomed as she sat at the kitchen table in her home. Mealtime in the Morgan household was a lively event, filled with the lively conversation of her parents and siblings, each eager to share stories about their day. Leanne uncovered the art of storytelling, becoming a master of its ebb and flow, the artful introduction and the gripping climax. She eagerly soaked up her mother's stories of daily encounters, her father's animated retellings of local happenings, and the lively banter that filled their home. Unbeknownst to her, she discovered herself sharing her own anecdotes, injecting a hint of amusement into the fabric of familial existence.

However, in the midst of all the laughter, there were also moments that tested her strength. Growing up as the daughter of a butcher in a charming Southern town came with its own set of challenges and expectations from society. Living in a rural area could sometimes feel stifling, as the traditional values of the community placed restrictions on a girl's aspirations, limiting her to the conventional roles of a wife and mother. However, these challenges also played a crucial role in shaping Leanne's quick sense of humor. She honed her skills in navigating through them with a sharp intellect that could disarm, a deep self-awareness that could diffuse any tension, and a steadfast determination to carve her own distinct path—despite the unknown that awaited her.

Leanne's sense of humor was shaped by her strong faith and the important role of the church in her community while she was growing up. The church was not just a place of worship; it functioned as a vibrant social center, where weekly performances of live comedy and drama took place. Leanne developed her skills in the art of timing, excelling in both comedic and spiritual aspects. She keenly observed the complex dynamics of human interactions during sermons, potlucks, and Sunday school gatherings. She experienced the incredible impact of laughter as a comforting balm, a means of healing and connecting, and as a graceful way to express sincerity. These early experiences with faith, community, and humor laid the groundwork for her comedic style, which would later resonate strongly with her audiences.

Looking back, it's clear that Leanne Morgan's path to comedy wasn't a planned endeavor, but rather a fortunate coincidence. Throughout her time in Tennessee, she acquired invaluable expertise in blending humor and sincerity, discovering delight in life's imperfections, and appreciating the impact of a captivating story. She never underwent any official training in comedy. Instead, she drew from her personal life experiences to discover humor in the mundane. She possessed a natural talent for observing the finer details and understood the strength of humor in overcoming challenges.

After years of honing her craft, Leanne confidently took the stage, showcasing her well-established and robust comedic roots. She had been sharing stories throughout her life, perfecting her storytelling skills in different settings such as the butcher shop, family gatherings, and her local church. This chapter of her life showcases how our origins can often unveil our genuine calling. Leanne Morgan's sense of humor blossomed during her formative years, as she embraced the warm and insightful atmosphere of her Southern community. This talent would later be shared with a worldwide audience.

CHAPTER 2

Jewelry Parties and Low-Rise Britches – The Unexpected Comedy School

Sometimes, the most valuable lessons can be discovered in unexpected places. Leanne Morgan's comedy career had a unique beginning, far from the usual open mic nights or exclusive performances in dimly lit clubs. Instead, it thrived in the living rooms of suburban women, amidst trays of finger sandwiches, glasses of sweet tea, and stunning displays of costume jewelry. These gatherings initially served as a way to sell jewelry and earn some additional income, but they unexpectedly evolved into a unique comedy training space. This experience formed the foundation for her unique style and ultimately propelled her onto bigger stages.

Leanne's foray into the world of direct sales was not motivated by a desire to pursue a career in comedy. Being a young wife and mother, she wanted to find a way to support her family financially while still being able to stay at home with her three children. Like many people in her situation, she chose to explore the "home party" business model, which provided the chance for a flexible income and potential growth. Little did she anticipate that these jewelry parties would provide the ideal opportunity for her to refine her comedic talents. Here, in the warm and relaxed environment of other women's homes, she found herself stepping up—not just selling jewelry, but captivating her audience with engaging stories.

The jewelry parties were, in many ways, a reflection of Leanne's future audience. The place was filled with vibrant individuals who appeared to be in a perpetual state of motion, effortlessly balancing the responsibilities of their careers, families, and personal well-being. These were individuals seeking a break from their everyday lives, even if only for a short while, and Leanne had a knack for offering them exactly that. She would proudly stand in front of them, wearing jewelry on her neck and wrists, and captivate her audience with her captivating stories. Her stories would center around her husband, Chuck, and their delightful everyday escapades. She would also share stories about the difficulties of raising children who always seemed to have a never-ending list of requests. Furthermore, she would share her personal experience of staying current with the latest trends, whether it be in diets or fashion. Her humor was rooted in everyday experiences, conveyed with an authentic and witty perspective that stems from personal understanding.

The jewelry was just the beginning attraction, but it was the fascinating stories that truly stole the spotlight. As she talked about her struggles with low-rise pants, a fashion trend that was all the rage in the early 2000s, she connected with a shared experience. Women in the audience would burst into laughter, nodding in agreement, as they too had experienced the struggle of fitting their bodies after childbirth into the latest fashion trend. Leanne's humor reflected the experiences of people, creating a sense of understanding and friendship instead of making fun. She appeared to grasp and accept the ridiculousness of the situation.

Leanne's comedic timing and storytelling skills thrived during these gatherings. Compared to the structured atmosphere of a comedy club, the jewelry parties offered her a more laid-back and authentic environment to test out fresh material. There was no set plan or predetermined structure—just Leanne, standing in a circle of women, improvising on whatever came to mind. She came to the realization that the key to successful comedy went beyond just the punchlines and required building genuine connections with others. She developed a keen ability to read the room, picking up on the energy of her audience, and adjusting her stories accordingly. If there was a specific subject that piqued her interest, she would explore it more deeply. If something didn't quite click, she would switch gears, always making sure her audience stayed engaged and entertained.

What started as a part-time pursuit quickly grew into something more significant. Leanne came to the realization that she wasn't just selling jewelry; she was providing people with the chance to experience a moment of escape, a refreshing breath of air, and an opportunity to laugh and let go. The parties became incredibly popular as word about them began to spread. Women were drawn to her, not just to buy jewelry, but also to arrange events solely to hear her speak. She brought immense joy and laughter to living rooms

38

across Tennessee, becoming the highlight of their week. With her clever disguise, she blended seamlessly into their group, effortlessly bringing laughter and joy. Leanne found herself immersed in a world where selling and storytelling intertwined, igniting a newfound passion within her.

Of course, there were some obstacles that arose during the process. Leanne's journey was filled with moments of uncertainty and self-doubt, especially when it came to finding a balance between her roles as a mother, wife, and aspiring comedian. She often faced the struggle of finding a delicate equilibrium between her passion for spreading happiness through comedy and the pressures of daily obligations. There were moments when she wondered if she was making the correct decision—if this diversion into comedy was merely a deviation from her true obligations. However, every time she saw the joy her stories brought to others and heard the genuine sound of laughter, she knew she had discovered something remarkable.

Leanne discovered the art of connecting with others through the jewelry parties. She had a unique style that set her apart from other Hollywood comedians. Instead, she was someone who could empathize with the challenges of feeling exhausted, overwhelmed, and disconnected from current trends. She delved into subjects that struck a chord with her audience: the perpetual quest for the perfect diet, the chaotic carpool queues, the highs and lows of matrimony, and the constant battle to find jeans that fit just right. She was a member of the group, facing challenges, persevering, and finding moments of levity along the way.

Leanne often shared amusing stories about her personal fashion mishaps, particularly the infamous low-rise pants, which quickly became a staple in her storytelling. The stories exuded a genuine and humble vibe. She would portray herself in a department store dressing room, struggling to squeeze into a pair of jeans that seemed to be designed for a much younger individual. As she made her way through the twists and turns, she couldn't help but find the entire situation ridiculous. The jeans were incredibly snug, making it difficult for her to breathe comfortably and causing her to make an effort to flatten her stomach. Eventually, she had to let go of fashion and focus on functionality. Her audience formed a strong emotional bond with her as they immersed themselves in her stories, relating to her frustrations and finding amusement in her exaggerated displays of defeat. This wasn't simply comedy; it was a shared experience.

Through these gatherings, Leanne discovered a newfound appreciation for the impact of her storytelling. She discovered that laughter possesses the ability to heal, bring people together, and lighten the burden of everyday challenges. Her humor was rooted in the genuine and relatable aspects of everyday life, finding joy in shared experiences and the imperfections that make life interesting.

When Leanne transitioned from hosting jewelry parties to performing in professional comedy venues, she already had a dedicated following of fans. These women had experienced her sense of humor directly and felt a real bond with her, as if she were a dear friend. They had observed her evolution from a jewelry saleswoman with a knack for storytelling to a talented comedian who could engage an audience with amusing anecdotes about Spanx or entertaining rants about Weight Watchers. The jewelry parties had served as her training ground, an unexpected comedy school where she refined her voice, polished her style, and built a connection with her audience.

When Leanne reflects on those early days, she frequently highlights that comedy seemed to find her, rather than her actively pursuing it. She was found in the living rooms of Tennessee, surrounded by a group of women who shared moments of both joy and sorrow. It found her during moments of true authenticity, when she openly discussed the absurdities and challenges of being a woman, a wife, a mother, and a friend.

Those jewelry parties revealed to her the genuine nature of comedy: it's more than just eliciting laughter, but about embodying authenticity, bravery, and fearlessly expressing thoughts that resonate with others. And for Leanne, that's where everything truly began.

CHAPTER 3

Hormones, Hiccups, and Humor –

Embracing the Adventure of Midlife

Midlife can occasionally take us by surprise, presenting a mix of possibilities, unease, and a new set of challenges. Leanne Morgan discovered that this stage of life offered plenty of material for her comedy, marking a significant turning point. While some may see perimenopause and the challenges of aging as a time to retreat and diminish, Leanne fully embraced it, displaying her unique humor, authenticity, and deep understanding of the human journey. Her stories about navigating hormonal changes, handling challenging people in their fifties, and surviving rock concerts in middle age are not just funny, but also offer comfort to anyone who has ever felt overwhelmed by the relentless march of time.

As Leanne approached her fifties, she found herself entering a new chapter in life, where the world around her appeared to be in a constant state of flux.

Her children were growing up and starting to live on their own, and she was entering a phase of life that is sometimes undervalued by society when it comes to women. However, instead of feeling unnoticed, Leanne experienced a passionate flame ignite within her. She saw this moment as an opportunity for self-reflection, self-reinvention, and reclaiming her narrative. What could have been a pivotal moment in life transformed into a fresh sense of direction. And what better way to fully embrace the complex journey of aging than by finding humor in it?

Leanne's comedy about this stage of life is remarkably relatable and genuine. One of her most popular routines explores the difficulties of dealing with perimenopausal symptoms, such as hot flashes, night sweats, mood swings, and the frustrating task of finding things in a purse the size of a small suitcase. Through her touch, these injustices take on a new form, becoming a shared experience that prompts women worldwide to reflect on the disappointments they've faced with their own bodies. She jokingly describes waking up drenched in sweat, feeling as if she's been in a fierce battle all night, only to realize it was just another episode of intense heat. She skillfully portrays the absurdity of trying to lead a conventional life while constantly being at the mercy of her unpredictable body.

However, her attention extends beyond the physical symptoms. Leanne explores the profound emotions commonly associated with this phase of life. She explores the occurrences of unexpected anger, where even the smallest annoyances, like a partner's loud breathing or a teenager's socks on the floor, can become intolerable. The way she openly expresses these emotions, with her usual cleverness, is truly invigorating. She inspires her audience to embrace their own quirks and find laughter in the ups and downs of life, acknowledging that our internal struggles can be just as surprising as the chaos around us.

Then there are people who display a clique mentality, reminiscent of our adolescent years, but now in the realm of adulthood. In her stand-up routine, Leanne humorously recounts her experience with a group of middle-aged women who appear to have never moved past their high school lunch table mentality. She playfully points out how they depend on Botox and designer handbags to uphold their appearance. She emphasizes the absurdity of mature women continuing to vie for social influence, engaging in gossip, and trying to outdo each other with their carefully curated lives. Leanne confidently brushes off the triviality of these social games, emphasizing their ongoing insignificance. She prioritizes authenticity over artificiality, empathy over cynicism, and a positive attitude over hostility.

Leanne explores the joys and challenges of rediscovering her identity as an individual, separate from her roles as a wife and mother. Throughout her life, her main focus was on caring for her children, being a strong support system for her husband, Chuck, and effectively managing the numerous responsibilities that come with running a household. However, as her children grew older and began to embark on their own paths, Leanne found herself facing a common question that many women face: "Who am I, apart from the different roles I've played?" Leanne embraced this as a thrilling adventure, rather than viewing it as a problem. She began to see herself as someone who had fully embraced change and was now ready to venture into uncharted territory.

Part of this exploration involved stepping beyond her familiar environment, sometimes quite literally. Leanne reflects on her fifties and how attending rock concerts has been a departure from the more calm and refined events she may have been accustomed to. She captures the mix of awe and bewilderment that comes from observing people her age rediscovering their youthful energy—dancing, shouting, and living as if they were in their twenties instead of their fifties. And while she may derive amusement from watching middle-aged individuals ignore caution (and their physical well-being), there is a profound appreciation for the idea of not allowing age to dictate our pursuit of happiness.

Her thoughts on these experiences are filled with a playful spirit, yet they also offer a sincere invitation: an invitation to live life with bravery and genuineness. She inspires her audience to embrace their true selves and conquer the fear of judgment. She encourages individuals to focus on their own well-being and not worry about what others think. Whether it's dancing at a concert or setting boundaries by saying "no," she inspires them to embrace their authenticity. She playfully comments on the freedom that comes with no longer being concerned about fitting into societal standards or meeting others' demands. "At some point," she laughs, "you realize that life is too short to put up with uncomfortable shoes or deal with difficult people."

Leanne's comedy is genuinely touching as she delves into the topics of getting older and the concept of beauty. Amidst a culture obsessed with staying young, she offers a refreshing perspective on embracing the natural changes that come with the passage of time. She openly talks about her "large flesh-colored underwear," using it as a lighthearted and charming metaphor for accepting and embracing one's body as it is, rather than trying to change it. She playfully mocks the beauty industry's obsession with "anti-aging" products, emphasizing the importance of embracing the natural process of aging as a journey to be cherished and celebrated. With a touch of humanity and a hint of authenticity, she encourages her audience to redirect their focus from the signs of aging and instead embrace the invaluable wisdom that accompanies life experience.

However, Leanne's reflections on midlife are characterized by a strong emphasis on finding happiness in the small moments. She explores the happiness that arises from discovering comfort in serene moments—enjoying a cup of coffee on the porch, immersing oneself in a captivating book, or cherishing the rare chance to sit undisturbed for a precious few minutes. She speaks of these moments with such genuine sincerity and appreciation that her audience can't help but feel a profound sense of gratitude for their own small moments of peace. Leanne's presence offers a calming influence in our fast-paced world, encouraging us to slow down, breathe deeply, and find joy in the little things.

Leanne Morgan's comedy about midlife embraces the highs and lows, the pleasures and obstacles of this phase of life, while acknowledging the realities of hot flashes or Botox. This season is a genuine and profound exploration of the chaotic and exquisite elements. It's crucial to acknowledge that aging is a precious chance, where every facial line tells a distinct story and every gray hair symbolizes wisdom and experience. She inspires her audience to discover joy in life's quirks, to value the insights they've acquired, and to cherish the instances of joy that arise from embracing their authentic selves rather than conforming to societal norms.

With a grin, she cheerfully remarks, "One of the advantages of getting older is having a decreased tolerance for foolishness." After years of putting others first, it's finally your moment to stand out. And what an amazing show it is—one filled with love, laughter, valuable lessons, and a wide range of vibrant experiences. In Leanne Morgan's world, embracing the joys and challenges of midlife is a constant source of laughter. She finds humor in the everyday chaos, making each day an adventure.

CHAPTER 4

Chuck and the Comedy of Love – Uncovering the Joy of Laughter in Marriage

Leanne Morgan's life and comedy are deeply shaped by her bond with her husband, Chuck. Their connection plays a crucial role in shaping her personal narrative and enhancing her on-stage charisma. Their marriage is a lovely blend of love, happiness, and the common challenges that many couples face but often keep to themselves. Leanne's sense of humor often reflects the dynamic of their relationship - a solid partnership founded on mutual support, a hint of playfulness, and a sincere appreciation for life's idiosyncrasies.

Leanne and Chuck's love story is anything but a fairy tale, yet it is undeniably captivating and genuine. They met in their charming Tennessee town, where Chuck's relaxed charm and serene demeanor perfectly complemented Leanne's vibrant and witty personality. Chuck truly valued and embraced

Leanne's sense of humor, even though they both had their own unique quirks. Their relationship is a wonderful illustration of how love can be remarkable even without flawlessness, as long as it is authentic.

Leanne's comedy frequently centers on the striking contrasts between her and Chuck. While Leanne is known for her lively and sharp sense of humor, Chuck is often portrayed as the laid-back counterpart. She teasingly comments on his knack for being both charming and exasperating, a man who thrives on simplicity but sometimes finds it challenging to grasp the complexities of her emotions. She fondly remembers Chuck's tendency to misunderstand the significance of certain life events or his comical obliviousness to the latest household chaos. Leanne's stand-up routines are brimming with a wealth of material, as she amusingly points out his lack of awareness.

Despite the playful banter, it's clear that Leanne and Chuck have a deep connection. Leanne's stories about Chuck go beyond playfully pointing out his imperfections and instead emphasize the ways he wholeheartedly supports and cherishes her. She discusses Chuck's dependability, his unwavering support of her professional aspirations, and his talent for injecting humor into her life, even during challenging times. Their bond, filled with shared laughter and unspoken understanding, stands as a testament to the strength of humor in maintaining a strong connection between partners amidst life's inevitable obstacles.

Leanne's comedy delves into the complexities of long-term marriage, capturing the unique quirks, daily routines, and occasional frustrations that shape a life shared between two individuals. She talks about how, throughout their marriage, Chuck's habits have evolved into a blend of amusement and annoyance. Chuck's quirks are depicted with a mix of affection and playful frustration, from his tendency to scatter dirty socks around the house to his unconventional approach to repairs. Leanne's ability to find humor in the everyday aspects of married life offers a relatable perspective for her audience, who often recognize their own partners in her descriptions.

One particularly touching aspect of Leanne's comedy is her reflection on how their relationship has evolved over time. She lightheartedly alludes to the shifts in their romantic journey—from the early stages of intense courtship to the settled, everyday rhythms of married life. She skillfully contrasts the exuberance of youth with the more established patterns of adulthood, highlighting the diverse ways in which love and romance can grow and thrive. Her stories about their evolving connection resonate with individuals who have experienced the transition from the thrill of fresh romance to the security of a lasting partnership.

Leanne's comedy about Chuck also emphasizes the importance of compromise and communication in marriage. She often shares anecdotes about the occasions when she and Chuck have had to navigate disagreements or find common ground. The stories are brimming with humor, while also expressing a profound admiration for the commitment needed to maintain a robust and harmonious connection. Leanne's candidness regarding their challenges, along with her ability to find humor in them, offers a refreshing perspective on the complexities of marriage.

Leanne's comedic portrayal of Chuck is truly remarkable, as she effortlessly captures the essence of their shared experiences. She recounts the various life challenges they've encountered as a team, from raising children to conquering unforeseen hurdles, always finding moments of levity amidst the hardships. Leanne highlights the ways in which their shared experiences have strengthened their bond, from their entertaining endeavors in home decoration to their collaborative culinary adventures (or lack thereof).

Leanne's comedy about Chuck also emphasizes the significance of discovering joy in our daily lives. She often brings up their daily rituals, like their Saturday morning routines or their serene evenings spent together on the porch. These moments, seemingly insignificant, are depicted as the heart of their connection. Leanne's sense of humor is a delightful celebration of the simple joys of everyday life and the warmth that comes from sharing those moments with someone special.

Leanne's comedy explores the theme of finding humor in relationships, while also sharing anecdotes about Chuck. She reflects on how humor can be a valuable asset for navigating the ups and downs of marriage. Her funny stories about Chuck and their relationship transcend mere amusement, showcasing the strong connection and resilience that emerge from facing life's challenges together. She demonstrates the power of humor in managing stress, fostering connections with loved ones, and maintaining optimism during challenging moments.

Leanne's perspective on marriage emphasizes the importance of maintaining a playful attitude as a couple. She emphasizes the significance of laughter in nurturing a vibrant and enduring relationship. Her ability to find humor in everyday situations, and her willingness to laugh at both the significant and trivial moments, highlights the significance of comedy in her life and marriage.

In the end, Leanne Morgan's comedy about her relationship with Chuck portrays a lovely image of a partnership built on love, laughter, and mutual respect. It's a celebration of the joys and challenges of marriage, portrayed with a lighthearted and authentic perspective. Leanne's stories are a gentle reminder that in the midst of life's chaos, there is always room for laughter. They also emphasize the significance of finding happiness in everyday moments, as these are the ones that genuinely enhance relationships.

CHAPTER 5

From Intimate Gatherings to the Grand Stage – A Journey of Joy and Impact

Leanne Morgan's incredible journey from hosting intimate jewelry parties to performing on grand stages in comedy clubs and arenas is a truly inspiring story of unwavering determination, remarkable personal growth, and the relentless pursuit of pure joy. This chapter delves into the incredible journey that took her from intimate local gatherings in

Tennessee to achieving widespread acclaim. It explores how she successfully navigated this transformation while staying true to her roots and preserving her unique comedic style.

The transition from selling jewelry at home parties to performing on stage didn't happen overnight. It required courage, determination, and a deep belief in her comedic intuition. Leanne's early performances in local clubs had a raw and unrefined quality, which stood in stark contrast to the polished routines she would later present. These initial experiences were marked by a series of small victories and important insights. Each performance was a chance for her to refine her material and engage with an audience who may not have been acquainted with her comedic style. She would face the typical challenges that come with pursuing a career in comedy: audiences that can be hard to predict, technical issues, and the occasional unsuccessful show. Nevertheless, Leanne confronted these challenges with the identical resolve and cleverness that characterized her performances.

The authenticity of her material greatly influenced her journey towards greater recognition. Leanne's comedy had a genuine and unique quality as she found inspiration in her personal life experiences, rather than relying on generic jokes or following trends. Her stories about perimenopause, her bond with Chuck, and her reflections on aging were not just funny observations; they were personal narratives that resonated with many people. Her genuine nature cultivated a strong connection with her audience, who appreciated her honesty and her ability to find humor in the obstacles of life. It also set her apart from others in the comedy world, allowing her to carve out a distinctive niche that was truly her own.

Leanne's achievements flourished as her reputation grew. Word of her performances rapidly spread, leading to increased recognition from larger venues and renowned media platforms. Her performances at comedy festivals and on national television showcases displayed her talent for captivating audiences with her unique blend of humor and genuine emotion. She honed her skills in crafting personal narratives into hilarious comedy that struck a chord with audiences, earning her a dedicated fan base and rave reviews from critics. With each new opportunity that presented itself, whether it was a late-night TV appearance or a larger comedy special, it became evident that her influence was growing and her distinctive comedic style was gaining power.

Despite her increasing popularity and more prominent public presence, Leanne remained grounded. She always stayed connected to her humble origins—the gatherings, the modest way of life, and the individuals who supported her from the start. The way she spoke about her journey and her interactions with fans highlighted her exceptional talent for fostering a deep connection. Leanne's genuine modesty and profound appreciation were apparent, and she often took moments to reflect on the people who had been there for her every step of the way. Her genuine nature connected deeply with her audience, reinforcing the idea that she was more than a comedian - she was a relatable person who had worked hard to achieve her aspirations.

As she continued to thrive, Leanne also prioritized giving back to the community. She passionately devoted herself to various charitable causes, using her comedic influence to raise awareness and support for important issues. Her commitment to creating a positive impact extended beyond her performances, demonstrating her faith in the transformative potential of humor. By organizing fundraisers, charity events, and sharing her personal experiences, Leanne demonstrated her commitment to making a positive impact on others, rather than solely pursuing personal gain.

Reflecting on her journey, Leanne's story is a powerful testament to the strength of dedication and authenticity. Her incredible journey, from selling jewelry locally to becoming a renowned comedian on a national scale, is a genuine testament to the strength of her passion, unwavering determination, and exceptional sense of humor. It's amazing how everyday experiences can turn into remarkable achievements. Leanne's ability to find humor in life's challenges, whether it's coping with hormonal changes or navigating the idiosyncrasies of marriage, has not only entertained but also provided inspiration for countless individuals.

Ultimately, Leanne Morgan's journey to success is a powerful example of the impact of comedy and the importance of staying true to oneself. Her story is truly inspiring for individuals who strive to make a meaningful difference in the world. It showcases the power of perseverance, authenticity, and embracing life's uncertainties to achieve one's goals and bring joy to others.

Leanne's humor and insights continue to connect with individuals, serving as a reminder of the joy that laughter brings and the positive impact it can have on ourselves and those around us.

CONCLUSION

Embracing the Laughs and Lessons

As we reach the conclusion of Leanne Morgan Prosopography: What in the World?! Essays and Inspirations by Leland Tyler invite deep contemplation of the remarkable journey that has been undertaken. Leanne Morgan's story is an extraordinary testament to the power of comedy, highlighting the profound influence of laughter, genuineness, and perseverance. Her journey from intimate gatherings to grand venues is a testament to the strength of discovering joy and meaning in the everyday moments of life.

Leanne's humor connects effortlessly with the genuine and relatable challenges of midlife, making it incredibly relatable. It's rooted in real-life experiences, which adds to its authenticity. Her wit and charm come alive as she lightheartedly points out the idiosyncrasies of perimenopause, the peculiarities of her husband Chuck, and the adventures that come with aging. She effortlessly brings laughter and provokes thought with her refreshing honesty. Her ability to turn life's obstacles into funny stories is a strong reminder of how valuable humor can be in navigating our own journeys.

Leanne's consistent authenticity is truly remarkable. In a world that often prioritizes projecting a meticulously constructed facade, Leanne offers a truly genuine and raw outlook on life. She exemplifies the value of not being overly serious, finding joy in our flaws, and embracing the unpredictability of life with a positive mindset. Her stories transcend mere humor, acting as a vehicle to establish connections through relatable experiences. They serve as a constant reminder of the shared experiences we encounter, both in times of struggle and in moments of triumph.

As we reflect on Leanne's journey, it serves as a poignant reminder of the importance of staying true to oneself. Her success can be attributed not only to her comedic talent, but also to her dedication to being genuine and relatable. It's a valuable lesson that goes far beyond the realm of comedy: significant accomplishments often come from being authentic and embracing our unique path.

Leanne's legacy is a wonderful combination of happiness and hope, along with resilience and positivity. Her journey exemplifies the incredible potential for personal growth and happiness that comes from embracing life's challenges and obstacles. As we face our own obstacles and navigate the ups and downs of life, it's comforting to realize that, like Leanne, we too can find amusement in chaos, connect with others through shared experiences, and approach each day with gratitude and happiness.

As we wrap up, let's keep embracing the essence of Leanne Morgan's comedy: a celebration of life's imperfections, a reminder to cherish the small moments, and an invitation to seek joy in our everyday experiences. May we all find our own paths to happiness, to create meaningful relationships, and to fully embrace our authentic selves, just as

Leanne has beautifully demonstrated. Here's to fully embracing the joyous moments, gaining wisdom from life's experiences, and wholeheartedly celebrating every step of Leanne Morgan's remarkable journey with humor and warmth.

Made in the USA
Middletown, DE
06 December 2024

66251002R00055